Mathew Brady

Leni Donlan

Chicago, Illinois

© 2008 Raintree
Published by Raintree,
A division of Reed Elsevier Inc.
Chicago, Illinois

Customer Service: **888-454-2279**

Visit our website at **www.raintreelibrary.com**

Designed by Kimberly R. Miracle and Betsy Wernert
Photo Research by Tracy Cummins
Map on page 29 by Mapping Specialists
Printed in China by Leo Paper Group

12 11 10 09 08
10 9 8 7 6 5 4 3 2 1

Library of Congress Cataloging-in-Publication Data
Donlan, Leni.
  Mathew Brady : photographing the Civil War / Leni Donlan.
      p. cm. -- (American history through primary sources)
  Includes bibliographical references and index.
  ISBN 978-1-4109-2699-9 (hardcover) -- ISBN 978-1-4109-2710-1 (pbk.)
  1. United States--History--Civil War, 1861-1865--Photography--Juvenile literature. 2. War photographers--United States--History--19th century--Juvenile literature. 3. Brady, Mathew B., 1823 (ca.)-1896--Juvenile literature. 4. Photographers--United States--Biography--Juvenile literature. 5. United States--History--Civil War, 1861-1865--Biography--Juvenile literature. I. Title.
  E468.7.D65 2008
  973.7'3092--dc22

                    2007005910

Acknowledgments
The author and publisher are grateful to the following for permission to reproduce copyright material: Library of Congress Geography and Map Division **pp. 5, 19 bottom, 27 bottom**; Library of Congress Prints and Photographs Division **pp. 6, 7, 8, 9, 10–11, 13, 14, 15, 16, 17, 18, 19 top, 20 top, 21, 22, 23, 24, 25, 26, 28, 29**; U.S. Army map **p. 12**; Getty Images **pp. 20 bottom** (Time Life Pictures), **27 top** (Rob Boudreau).

Cover photograph of Mathew Brady returned from Bull Run reproduced with permission of the Library of Congress Prints and Photographs Division.

Every effort has been made to contact copyright holders of any material reproduced in this book. Any omissions will be rectified in subsequent printings if notice is given to the publishers.

Disclaimer
All the Internet addresses (URLs) given in this book were valid at the time of going to press. However, due to the dynamic nature of the Internet, some addresses may have changed, or sites may have changed or ceased to exist since publication. While the author and publishers regret any inconvenience this may cause readers, no responsibility for any such changes can be accepted by either the author or the publishers.

It is recommended that adults supervise children on the Internet.

Contents

Some words are printed in bold, **like this**. You can find out what they mean on page 30. You can also look in the box at the bottom of the page where they first appear.

A House Divided

In the 1800s, there were many changes in the United States. In the northern states, cities grew. Businesses grew.

In the southern states, **plantations** were the center of life. Plantations were large farms. White men owned the plantations. They also owned black slaves. Slaves were told what to do. They did all of the work.

People in the North wanted to stop **slavery**. Slavery is when someone (a slave) is owned by another person. They are told what to do and how to live. But people in the South wanted to keep slavery. Plantation owners could not run their plantations without slaves.

The American Civil War

THE TWO SIDES:	
The United States of America	The Confederate States of America
THE ARMIES WERE CALLED:	
Federal, Blue, U.S., Yankee	Confederacy, Gray, Rebel
LEADERS:	
President Abraham Lincoln	President Jefferson Davis
UNIFORM COLOR:	
Blue	Gray
REASON FOR FIGHTING:	
To keep the country together; to stop slavery	To protect the plantation way of life; to own slaves

civil war	when two sides of the same country fight
plantation	large farm that used slaves
secede	move out of; stop being a part of
slavery	when someone is under the control of or owned by another person

1ˢ BACON'S MILITARY MAP OF AMERICA. 1ˢ

BACON'S
MILITARY MAP OF THE
UNITED STATES
Showing the
FORTS & FORTIFICATIONS.
Published by BACON & Co Newman Str.
LONDON 1862

This is a map of the United States. It shows the country in the years from 1860 to 1863. The pink and yellow states had slaves. So did the territories.

So the southern states decided to keep slavery. They wanted to **secede** or stop being part of the United States. The president (leader) of the United States was Abraham Lincoln. He and others wanted the North and South to stick together.

Lincoln said, "A house divided cannot stand." In 1861 the "house," meaning the country, divided. The American **Civil War** began. A civil war is when two sides from the same country fight.

Introducing Mathew Brady

Many people have written about the American **Civil War**. But one man told his story with **photographs**. He took pictures of the Civil War. That photographer was Mathew Brady.

This is a group of artists. Mathew Brady is in the front row on the left.

New York City looked like this when Brady lived there.

photograph   picture made with a camera. A photographer is someone who takes pictures.

telegraph   system for sending messages by a code over wires

Brady was born in the state of New York in 1823. His parents were farmers. Brady left home when he was sixteen years old. He moved to New York City. Brady met many artists there. One of these artists was Samuel F. B. Morse. Morse was also an inventor. Morse taught Brady photography. Photography is the art of making pictures with a camera. Photography changed Brady's life.

This is a photograph of Samuel F. B. Morse. Mathew Brady took the photograph.

Samuel F. B. Morse is best known for a famous invention. It was the **telegraph**. The telegraph is a system that sends messages over wires. It uses dots and dashes to spell out words. The telegraph was an important tool during the Civil War.

Brady of Broadway

In 1844 Brady opened his own **studio**. A studio is the place where a **photographer** works. Brady photographed many people. He took pictures of presidents and writers. He took pictures of actors and other famous people. These people were the stars of his time. Many people came to see Brady's photographs. They were called his **Gallery** (collection of photographs) of Stars. Brady was now known as "Brady of Broadway." Broadway is a famous street in New York City. His studio was there. He was rich and famous. He was living his dream.

This picture was in a newspaper. It shows Mathew Brady's famous gallery. He hung his photographs there. The gallery was in New York City.

gallery   long, narrow room used to show artwork; also used to mean a collection of artwork

studio   place where a photographer works

Brady took this photograph of Abraham Lincoln in 1860. About 100 photographs were taken of Lincoln. Brady took almost one-third of all of them.

Brady opened two more studios. One was in New York City. The other was in Washington, D.C. By then, the American **Civil War** had started. Brady wanted to photograph the war. He hired many photographers to work with him.

Brady believed he was more than an artist. He knew that photographs were an important way to show history. Brady believed it was his duty to photograph the war.

"A spirit in my feet said, 'Go,' and I went"

Brady and his staff took pictures of the American **Civil War** for four years. They **photographed** places where battles were fought. They photographed **destruction**. This shows what was left after things have been destroyed by the war. They photographed **injury** (hurt or loss) and death. They photographed weapons. They photographed life in army camps. And they photographed the soldiers. Later, Brady explained: "I had to go. A spirit in my feet said, 'Go,' and I went."

Brady took very few Civil War photographs himself. But he planned and led the work of other photographers. Many Civil War photographs have "Photograph by Brady" printed on them. Brady might not have taken all the photographs. But he gathered and **preserved** them. He kept them safe.

Rolling darkrooms

During the Civil War, photographers brought cameras and **darkrooms** with them. A darkroom is a space that blocks all light. It took photographers a long time to take a photograph. So, cameras of the 1860s could not take "action" photographs. Most of the pictures of battles were drawings by artists.

darkroom room or space that blocks all light and is used in photography
destruction act of destroying something; also used to mean what is left after something is destroyed

This team of photographers has their camera in the wagon. The wagon is their darkroom, too.

11

Seeing the American Civil War

The first gunshots of the American **Civil War** were fired over Fort Sumter. This was in Charleston, South Carolina. It was April, 1861. But the first battle of the war came months later.

Battle of Bull Run, July 21, 1861

Location

Fairfax County and
Prince William County, Virginia

Result Confederate victory

Sides

United States of America
Confederate States of America

Killed

460
387

Wounded

1,124
1,582

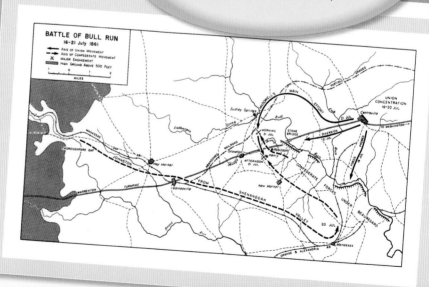

This map shows Bull Run. It is in the state of Virginia. This is where the first battle of the Civil War took place.

Confederate   part of the United States led by President Jefferson Davis during the American Civil War. These eleven southern states wanted to keep slavery.

Union   part of the United States led by President Abraham Lincoln during the

This is a photo of Mathew Brady. He was at the Battle of Bull Run all day.

It happened on July 21, 1861 in northern Virginia. Many people traveled from Washington, D.C. to see the battle. People acted like the battle was a sports event!

There were two armies. The **Union** army was from the northern states. The **Confederate** army was from the southern states. Most people thought the Union army would win the battle. They thought the Union army would quickly win the whole war.

The Union Army did seem to be winning early in the day. Then things changed. The Union soldiers fought the Confederate soldiers up a hill. But more and more Confederate soldiers joined to help. They became strong again. Union soldiers started to run. Many were taken as prisoners. Many died. The Union lost the battle.

This battle was called the Battle of Bull Run. After the Battle of Bull Run, no one knew what to expect. They did know that they should prepare for a long war.

This man and woman have just returned from the Battle of Bull Run.

More battles

On March 9, 1862, two warships fought. They were the *Monitor* and *Merrimack*. It was called the Battle of the Monitor and the Merrimack. The *Monitor* was a **Union** ship. The *Merrimack* was a **Confederate** ship. They fought near Hampton Road, Virginia. Neither side had a real win in this battle.

On April 6, 1862, the Battle of Shiloh was fought in Tennessee. About 13,000 Union soldiers were killed or wounded. About 10,000 Confederate soldiers were killed or **wounded**. More soldiers were killed or wounded here than in all earlier U.S. wars combined!

Professor Thaddeus S. C. Lowe led the Union Army Balloon Corps. He used hot-air balloons to spy on the Confederate Army.

wound   break to skin, bones, or other body parts from a fight or a battle in war

This painting shows the Battle of the Monitor and Merrimack. It was the first fight between iron warships.

The Battle of Seven Pines followed. It was fought from May 31 to June 1, 1862. It was fought in Fair Oaks, Virginia. Neither army had a real win in this battle, either.

In late August 1862 the Second Battle of Bull Run took place. The Confederate Army won this battle. Over 4,000 Union soldiers were captured or missing.

Brady's **photographers** continued to follow the war. They knew they were recording history.

A boys' war

Some people call the American **Civil War** the Boys' War. Many of the soldiers were 21 years old or younger. Boys as young as thirteen years old were in the war. Many of the very young soldiers were drummer boys. They did not carry weapons. But even some drummer boys were killed or **wounded** during the war.

This is a photo of an outdoor hospital. **Wounded** soldiers came here directly from battle.

This doctor is working on a soldier's dead body. Then it can be sent to the soldier's family for burial.

16

veteran person who has actively served his or her country as a soldier

Johnny Clem may have been the youngest soldier in the Civil War. He was only ten years old when he became a drummer boy! Clem's drum was smashed at the Battle of Shiloh. A year later, Clem had his own gun. He was fighting in the battle of Chickamauga in Tennessee. Johnny became famous when he killed a **Confederate** soldier. Johnny is remembered as the Drummer Boy of Chickamauga.

Almost 600,000 people died in the Civil War. More than 400,000 soldiers were injured. Sadly, the largest losses were among the youngest soldiers. After the war, many young **veterans** had problems from illness or injury. Veterans are people who had been soldiers. These problems lasted for many years.

Many boys lied about their age so they could join the army. Other young soldiers were able to join the army as drummer boys.

A bloody battle

September 17, 1862, was the bloodiest day yet in the American **Civil War**. It was the Battle of Antietam. Antietam is in the state of Maryland. More than 4,800 **Union** and **Confederate** soldiers were killed. Around 18,000 were **wounded**.

This was the first big battle that took place outside of Confederate states. It was not a clear win for the Union Army. But the Confederate Army was pushed back into Confederate states.

President Lincoln felt the battle showed that the Union would win the war. Lincoln spoke to the people of the United States. The date was September 22, 1862. He talked about his plan to **emancipate** the slaves. He was going to free all of the slaves in the Confederate states.

Allan Pinkerton (left), President Abraham Lincoln (middle), and Major General John A. McClernand (right) visit Antietam on October 3, 1862. Pinkerton was head of the Union **Intelligence Service**. He worked to gather secrets about the Confederate Army. McClernand was an officer during the Civil War.

intelligence service   group of people that gathers information about an enemy
emancipate   free from slavery

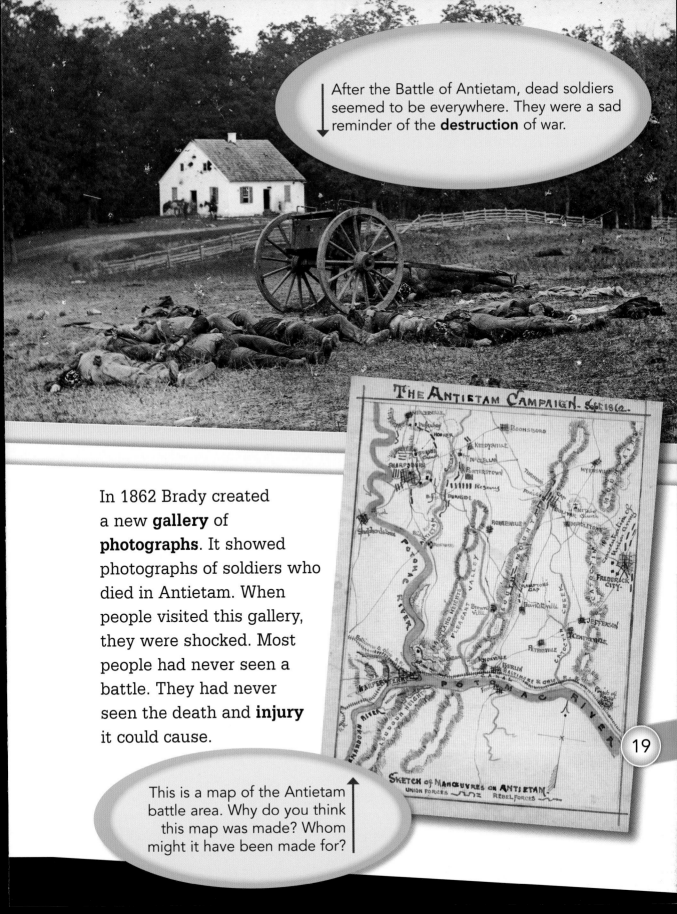

After the Battle of Antietam, dead soldiers seemed to be everywhere. They were a sad reminder of the **destruction** of war.

In 1862 Brady created a new **gallery** of **photographs**. It showed photographs of soldiers who died in Antietam. When people visited this gallery, they were shocked. Most people had never seen a battle. They had never seen the death and **injury** it could cause.

This is a map of the Antietam battle area. Why do you think this map was made? Whom might it have been made for?

Many dead

Gettysburg is in Pennsylvania. Pennsylvania is a **Union** state. The Battle of Gettysburg was fought from July 1 to July 3, 1863. Once again, the **Confederate** Army had decided to fight outside the Confederate states. This battle was the real turning point of the war.

Around 160,000 Union and Confederate soldiers fought in this battle. More than 51,000 soldiers died. Close to 8,000 died on the **battlefield**. They died right where they fought. The rest died from their **wounds**.

This is the artist Alfred Waud. He was able to draw the action that the camera could not capture. He is sketching the Gettysburg battlefield.

This is Abraham's Lincoln's handwritten speech. Do you think he knew how important this speech would become?

battlefield   place where a battle is fought or was once fought
in vain   for no good reason

Alfred Waud sketched this scene from the Battle of Gettysburg.

The Union Army took control of Gettysburg after three days of fighting. The Confederate Army went back to Virginia. Gettysburg was left a terrible mess.

The bodies of dead soldiers were lying in the hot summer sun. They needed to be buried quickly. Over 3,000 horses died in the battle. Their bodies were burned in large piles. The smell in Gettysburg was very bad. Many people became sick. The **destruction** of the war could still be seen months later. On November 19, President Abraham Lincoln gave his Gettysburg Address. This speech reminded the country of the effort needed to finish the war. It reminded the country that no soldier in this war had died **in vain**. They died for a good reason.

An awful prison

About 150 prisons were built during the American **Civil War**. In the first few years of the war, the armies traded prisoners. Soldiers were not in prison very long. In 1863 they stopped trading prisoners. The Confederate states refused to trade black prisoners.

In November 1863, the Confederate Army opened a new prison. It was in Andersonville, Georgia. Prisoners began arriving in February 1864.

The prison was terrible. Prisoners had to provide their own shelter from the weather. Soldiers died of disease and **starvation**. They did not have enough to eat. The water was not safe to drink. In one year, more than 13,000 of them died there.

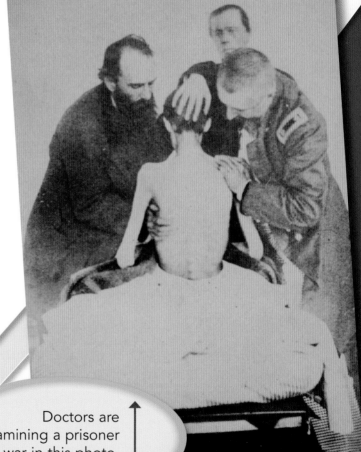

Doctors are examining a prisoner of war in this photo.

arrest   captured by police
starvation   becoming sick from not having enough food to eat

Here, Henry Wirz is about to be hanged.

Henry Wirz was in charge of Andersonville Prison. After the war, Wirz was **arrested**. He was captured by police. He was charged with planning to "**injure** the health and destroy the lives of soldiers … of the United States." Wirz was found guilty. His punishment was death by hanging.

Can the Camera Lie?

Have you heard the saying "the camera never lies?" It is true. The camera cannot lie. It just records what is in front of it. However, a **photographer** can control how a photograph looks.

Photographers can choose how to take their photographs. They can even add things or move things in a photograph. They can add a weapon or clothing. Photographers can use words to explain their photographs, too. Some photographers do all of these things. Why? So that the **viewers** will see what the photographer wants them to see. The viewers are the people looking at the photo.

This photograph appeared in a book by Alexander Gardner. Gardner said these were dead Confederate soldiers.

traitor   person who cannot be trusted; person who acts to hurt his or her country
viewer   person who looks at something or some event

This picture appeared in the same book. Gardner said these were dead Union soldiers.

One American **Civil War** photographer was Timothy O'Sullivan. He used the same **scene** to tell two different stories! A man named Alexander Gardner used his photos in a book. Gardner called one photograph "Harvest of Death" (left). It shows dead **Confederate** soldiers from the Battle of Gettysburg. He called the dead soldiers **traitors** to their country. A traitor acts against his or her country.

Then, Gardner showed O'Sullivan's other photograph from the Battle of Gettysburg (above). He said this photograph showed **Union** soldiers who died in battle. He called these dead soldiers heroes.

Several clues show that the photographs are two views of the same scene. The photographs were taken from different sides.

Look closely. Can you see that the camera did not lie? Alexander Gardner did!

25

Mathew Brady: After the War

Brady spent almost all of his money on photographing the Civil War. He was no longer rich when the war ended. He was no longer "Brady of Broadway," photographer of the stars. While he was away taking war photographs, other photographers had become famous.

People wanted to forget the terrible war. No one wanted to buy Brady's war **photographs**. In 1875 the U.S. government finally bought Brady's photographs. They paid $25,000. Brady used that money to pay his debts. He had to pay many people money he owed them. When Brady died in 1896, he was very poor.

This picture of Brady was taken a few years before he died.

debt	money owed (that must be paid) to others
photojournalist	photographer who tells news stories mostly through photographs
reality	something that is true; the truth

Brady thought he was forgotten. He was wrong. He was buried at Arlington Cemetery in Virginia. This is an important cemetery where soldiers are buried. He was buried among the American **Civil War** heroes he had photographed.

Mathew Brady changed the art of photography. His work during the Civil War led the way for future **photojournalists**. These are photographers who tell news stories through photographs. Today, people still understand the Civil War through Brady's photographs. Brady is remembered as an artist. He helped to **preserve** (save) the history of the Civil War.

Arlington Cemetery, Virginia.

"Mr. Mathew Brady has done something to bring us the terrible reality [truth] … of the war. If he has not brought bodies and laid them in our door-yards and along our streets, he has done something very like it."
—the New York Times, 1862

Timeline of the American Civil War

Jefferson Davis

This picture was taken March 4, 1861. It shows a crowd gathering to see Lincoln become president.

Battle of Shiloh

1861

January 1861:	The South **secedes** from the United States.
February 1861:	Jefferson Davis become president of the **Confederate** states.
March 1861:	Abraham Lincoln becomes president of the United States.
April 1861:	First shots of the American **Civil War** are fired at Fort Sumter in Charleston, South Carolina.
April 1861:	Richmond, Virginia, becomes the Confederate **capital.**
July 1861:	First Battle of Bull Run is fought.

1862

January 1862:	Abraham Lincoln orders the **Union** Army to take action.
March 1862:	Battle of the Monitor and Merrimack is fought.
April 1862:	Battle of Shiloh is fought.
September 1862:	Battle of Antietam is fought.

1863

January 1863:	President Lincoln orders to free all slaves.
June–July 1863:	Gettysburg Campaign is fought.
September 1863:	Battle of Chickamauga is fought.

assassinate	kill a political leader
capital	location of the government
surrender	to give up, as in a battle

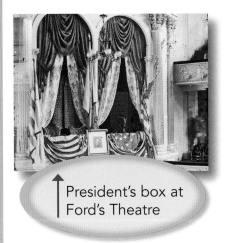

President's box at Ford's Theatre

1864

May 1864: Battle of Spotsylvania is fought. More than 27,000 soldiers were killed.

1865

April 1865: Confederate leader Robert E. Lee **surrenders** (gives up). The Civil War is over.

April 1865: President Lincoln is **assassinated** (murdered).

November 1865: Captain Henry Wirz is hanged.

This map shows all the battles and other places mentioned in this book. There were many other battles in the Civil War, too.

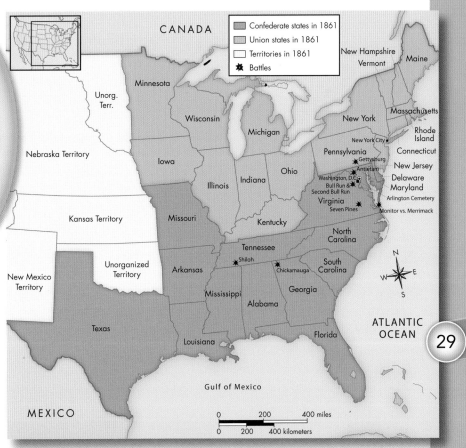

CANADA

- Confederate states in 1861
- Union states in 1861
- Territories in 1861
- Battles

New Hampshire
Vermont
Maine
Minnesota
Unorg. Terr.
Wisconsin
Michigan
New York
Massachusetts
Rhode Island
New York City
Nebraska Territory
Iowa
Pennsylvania
Connecticut
Gettysburg
Antietam
New Jersey
Ohio
Indiana
Washington, D.C.
Delaware
Illinois
Bull Run & Second Bull Run
Maryland
Virginia
Arlington Cemetery
Seven Pines
Monitor vs. Merrimack
Kansas Territory
Missouri
Kentucky
North Carolina
Tennessee
Unorganized Territory
Arkansas
Shiloh
Chickamauga
South Carolina
New Mexico Territory
Georgia
Mississippi
Alabama
ATLANTIC OCEAN
Texas
Florida
Louisiana

N
W E
S

Gulf of Mexico

MEXICO

0   200   400 miles
0   200   400 kilometers

Glossary

civil war when two sides of the same country fight. The American Civil War was fought between 1861 and 1865.

assassinate kill a political leader

battlefield place where a battle is fought or was once fought

capital location of the governement

Confederate part of the United States led by President Jefferson Davis during the American Civil War. These eleven southern states wanted to keep slavery.

darkroom room or space that blocks all light and is used in photography

debt money owed (that must be paid) to others

destruction act of destroying something; also used to mean what is left after something is destroyed

emancipate free from slavery

gallery long, narrow room used to show artwork; also used to mean a collection of artwork

in vain for no good reason

injury hurt or loss

intelligence service group of people who gathers information and secrets on enemies

photograph picture made with a camera. A photographer is someone who takes pictures.

photojournalist photographer who tells news stories mostly through photographs

plantation large farm that used slaves

preserve keep or save from injury or loss

reality something that is true; the truth

secede move out of; stop being a part of

slavery when someone is under the control of or owned by another person

starvation becoming sick from not having enough food to eat

studio place where a photographer works

surrender give up, as in a battle

telegraph electric system for sending messages by a code over wires

traitor person who cannot be trusted; person who acts to hurt his or her country

Union part of the United States led by President Abraham Lincoln during the American Civil War. The Union wanted to end slavery.

veteran person who has actively served his or her country as a soldier

viewer person who looks at something or some event

wound break to skin, bones, or other body parts from a fight or a battle in war

Want to Know More?

Books to read

- Armstrong, Jennnifer. *Photo by Brady: A Picture of the Civil War*. New York: Antheneum, 2005.

- Pfluger, Lynda. *Mathew Brady: Photographer of the Civil War*. New Jersey: Enslow, 2001.

- Wisler, G. Clifton. *Mr. Lincoln's Drummer*. New York: Lodestar, 1995.

Websites

- **Selected Civil War Photographs**
  http://memory.loc.gov/ammem/cwphtml/cwphome.html

- **Civil War Maps: 1861–1865**
  http://memory.loc.gov/ammem/collections/civil_war_maps/

Places to visit

- **Arlington National Cemetery**
  Arlington, VA 22211
  (703) 607-8000

- **Gettysburg National Military Park**
  97 Taneytown Road
  Gettysburg, PA 17324
  (717) 334-1124 ext. 431

Read *Route 66: America's Road* to find out about this historic road and the many sites along it.

Read *Strike It Rich in Cripple Creek: Gold Rush* to find out why people rushed to the West during the mid-1800s.

Index